PRINCIPLES
OF
PERSONAL DEFENSE

PRINCIPLES
OF
PERSONAL
DEFENSE

BY
JEFF COOPER

Foreword by Louis Awerbuck

Illustrated by Paul Kirchner

PALADIN PRESS
BOULDER, COLORADO

Also by Jeff Cooper:

The Art of the Rifle
The Art of the Rifle: Special Color Edition
C Stories
Fireworks: A Gunsite Anthology
To Ride, Shoot Straight, and Speak the Truth

CONTENTS

FOREWORD

There are two men who influenced my life more than any other — my late father and Jeff Cooper.

I have had the privilege of knowing Colonel Cooper for three decades, during which time he has filled the roles of mentor, teacher, counsellor, and friend. Without the benefit of his teachings I would probably not be alive today — and neither would many others.

The greatest testament to his life's work is the fact that currently there is not one firearms instructor of repute who was not influenced one way or another by his freely passed-on knowledge. A man of honor and integrity, he expects no less of others, and that is why he commands respect. In a day and age when almost anything can be bought, respect is the one quality which still has to be earned — and he has earned it.

In the early 1980s, when Jeff and Janelle paid my salary, I was never treated like an employee, and always felt I was working *with* the Coopers, as opposed to working *for* them. I was informed what needed to be done to facilitate the smooth running of Orange Gunsite during those Glory Days, and I did it. It was as simple as that, and that's the way it should be.

Of all his prolific writings spanning half a century, including *Cooper on Handguns,* books on the "how-to's" of sports car driving, Old West gunfighters, and later works such as *Fireworks* and *To Ride, Shoot Straight, and Speak the Truth,* the one which intrigued me more than any other was also the shortest. This was the original *Principles of Personal Defense.*

When all is said and done — as has been stated so many times through history — the mind is more important than any mechanical weapon. An armed idiot savant could be a dangerous enemy, but an armed idiot with no savant may as well be unarmed. He's just another idiot.

And this is the gist of Colonel Cooper's *Principles of Personal Defense.*

It is a classic, timeless work, encapsulated in a clear, concise, and succinct form. And like a twentieth-century Western Civilization equivalent of Musashi's seventeenth-century *Book of Five Rings,* it should be read, studied, and then periodically reread and restudied. No matter how many times you read it, you will always find one more pearl of wisdom that you missed during the last read.

Principles of Personal Defense is the fighting man's guide to mental conditioning — plain and simple. And there is no better work on the subject — period.

Maybe the Glory Days are gone, and Baby's throaty roar no longer rings out over the Yavapai hills, but the wisdom and knowledge are laid out in print for perpetuity. All you have to do is read and learn . . .

Louis Awerbuck
January 2006

PREFACE

It is not common for an author to enjoy rereading something that he wrote a decade previously. Times change, styles change, attitudes change, and most of all people grow, both intellectually and emotionally. It is therefore with gratification and some little surprise that I was able to reread *Principles of Personal Defense* and to discover that I felt no need to change anything of importance. It stands as it stood, and insofar as it spoke the truth years ago, it speaks it still.

The booklet is essentially a digest of a presentation I developed while working in Nicaragua (before the Communist takeover there). This part of the world has always been turbulent, and the need for individual self-defense has remained fairly constant ever since the departure of the Spanish in the early part of the nineteenth century. Individual conduct in lethal confrontation is not, however, something that is confined to any one locale or era, and if there are principles guiding its conduct — and I believe there are — those principles do not change according to geography, history, or sociological whim. If a principle exists it must be immutable, for that is what a principle is — a truth standing apart from the mood of the times.

If I were to rewrite this pamphlet completely, the only thing I would change would be those few personal anecdotes that appear within it. I would update them to include only those that have taken place within the last year or so. As it now stands, the anecdotes are all at least twenty years old, but the more I look at them, the more I realize that there is no need to change them, because the experiences that have more recently come across my desk, and in which I have lately been involved, simply corroborate what has already been set down. These experiences could be rewritten to include nothing that happened more than one year ago and we would have the same story. Thus it has not been necessary to do any extensive rewriting.

To emphasize this point, however, should mention that only this last week another episode came to my attention that was immensely satisfying in its exemplification of several of the principles set forth in this work. It seems a yachtsman was asleep in his power cruiser docked in the Bahamas. After midnight he opened his eyes to be aware of two intruders inhis cabin, one of whom was pointing a Mini-14 at his chest from a range of abouteighteen inches. This is a startling situation. This is an intimidating situation. It might properly be termed a terrifying situation. But the man remembered his principles and instantly attacked, with his hands, and won. He personified the principles of decisiveness, aggressiveness, speed, and surprise in a most satisfactory manner.

Stories such as this come to my attention with such frequency that it would take a whole directory to list them. They establish beyond any question that the principles we have taught over the decades (and still continue to teach at Gunsite) are valid beyond any contradiction. Our work here is conducted in order to keep the victims of aggression alive, and the knowledge that it succeeds is our reward.

Principles of Personal Defense has been received with only moderate enthusiasm by the law enforcement establishment. Several departments have adopted it, but only with the deletion of the principles of aggressiveness and ruthlessness. It obviously makes for bad press to have a department known as both aggressive and ruthless. This is quite understandable, but it does not invalidate the principles. In war there is no substitute for victory, and this is equally true of personal combat, which is, after all, a microcosm of war. When a coward is offered deadly violence, his reaction may be to surrender, or cower, or flee, or call for help; not one of these choices is likely to obviate his peril.

But this booklet was not written for cowards.

INTRODUCTION

Some people prey upon other people. Whether we like it or not, this is one of the facts of life. It has always been so and it is not going to change. The number of sociopaths in a stipulated population varies widely, but we can take a figure of one in one hundred, for simplicity's sake, and not be far off. About one person in one hundred will, under some circumstances, initiate a violent attack upon another, in defiance of the law, for reasons that seem sufficient to him at the time. Take the able-bodied male population of your community, divide it by one hundred, and you have a fair approximation of the number of possible contacts who just might take it upon themselves to beat your head in. It is not pertinent to dispute the mathematics of this calculation. It may be wrong for your place and time. But anyone who is aware of his environment knows that the peril of physical assault does exist, and that it exists everywhere and at all times. The police, furthermore, can protect you from it only occasionally.

The author assumes that the right of self-defense exists. Some people do not. This booklet is not for them. This is for those who feel that anyone who chooses physically to attack another human being does so at his peril. In some jurisdictions it is held that the victim of an attacker must, above all, attempt to escape. This is a nice legalistic concept, but it is very often tactically unsound. By the time one has exhausted every means of avoiding conflict it may be too late to save his life. Laws vary, and cannot be memorized encyclopedically; in any case, we are not concerned here about jurisprudence — but about survival. If one lives through a fight, we will assume that he is better off than if he does not, even though he may be thereafter confronted with legal action.

Violent crime is feasible only if its victims are cowards. A victim who fights back makes the whole business impractical. It is true that a victim who fights back may suffer for it, but one who does not almost certainly *will* suffer for it. And, suffer or not, the one who fights back retains his dignity and his self-respect. Any study of the atrocity list of recent years — Starkweather, Speck, Manson, Richard Hickok, and Cary Smith, et al — shows immediately that the victims, by their appalling ineptitude and timidity, virtually assisted in their own murders. ("Don't make them mad, Martha, so they won't hurt us.")

Any man who is a man may not, in honor, submit to threats or violence. But many men who are not cowards are simply unprepared for the fact of human savagery. They have not thought about it (incredible as this may appear to anyone who reads the paper or listens to the news) and they just don't know what to do. When they look right into the face of depravity or violence, they are astonished and confounded. This can be corrected.

The *techniques* of personal combat are not covered in this work. The so-called "martial arts" (boxing, karate, the stick, the pistol, etc.) are complete studies in themselves and must be acquired through suitable programs of instruction, training, and practice. It behooves all able-bodied men and women to consider them. But the subject of this work is more basic than technique, being a study of the guiding *principles* of survival in the face of unprovoked violence on the part of extralegal human assailants. Strategy and tactics are subordinate to the principles of war, just as individual defensive combat is subordinate to the following principles of personal defense.

ALERTNESS

PAUL KIRCHNER ©2005

Principle One:
ALERTNESS

"**A** commander may be forgiven for being defeated, but never for being surprised." This maxim is among the first to be impressed upon new lieutenants. It is equally applicable to individuals who aspire to a degree of physical security in today's embattled society. Alertness is, to some extent, an inherent personality trait, but it can nonetheless be learned and improved. Once we accept that our familiar and prosaic environment is in fact perilous, we automatically sharpen our senses.

Two rules are immediately evident: Know what is behind you, and pay particular attention to anything out of place.

It is axiomatic that the most likely direction of attack is from behind. Be aware of that. Develop "eyes in the back of your head." Eric Hartmann, the World War II German flying ace who is possibly the greatest fighter pilot of all time (1,405 combat missions, 352 confirmed victories), felt that he survived because of an "extremely sensitive back to his neck"; and, conversely, claimed that 80 percent of his victims never knew he was in the same sky with them. Combat flying is not the same as personal defense, but the principle applies. The great majority of the victims of violent crime are taken by surprise. The one who anticipates the action wins. The one who does not, loses. Learn from the experience of others and *don't let yourself be surprised*.

Make it a game. Keep a chart. Every time anyone is able to approach you from behind without your knowledge, mark down an X. Every time you see anyone you know before he sees you, mark down an O. Keep the Os ahead of the Xs. A month with no Xs establishes the formation of correct habits.

Observe your cat. It is difficult to surprise him. Why? Naturally his superior hearing is part of the answer, but not all of it. He moves well, using his senses fully.

He is not preoccupied with irrelevancies. He's not thinking about his job or his image or his income tax. He is putting first things first, principally his physical security. Do likewise.

There are those who will object to the mood this instruction generates. They will complain that they do not wish to "live like that." They are under no obligation to do so. They can give up. But it is a feral world, and if one wishes to be at ease in it one must accommodate to it.

Anything out of place can be a danger signal. Certainly anyone you don't know approaching your dwelling must be regarded askance. It's ninety-nine to one that he is perfectly harmless, but will you be ready if he turns out to be that other one who is not?

Certain things are obvious: an unfamiliar car parked across the street for long periods with people in it who do not get out; a car that maintains a constant distance behind you while you vary your speed; young men in groups, without women, staying in one place and not talking. These things should set off a first-stage alarm in anyone, but there are many other signals to be read by the wary. Anyone who appears to be triggered out of watchfulness and into action by your appearance must be explained. Anyone observing you carefully must be explained. Anyone whose behavior seems to be geared to yours must be explained. If the explanation does not satisfy you, be ready to take appropriate defensive action.

A common ruse of the sociopath is the penetration of a dwelling under false pretenses. Anyone can claim to be a repairman or an inspector of one sort or another. It is often impractical to verify credentials, but merely being aware that credentials may easily be falsified is protection against surprise. The strong need only remain watchful. The weak should take further precautions.

On the street, let no stranger take your hand. To allow a potential assailant a firm grip on your right hand is to give him a possibly fatal advantage. Use your eyes. Do not enter unfamiliar areas that you cannot observe first. Make it a practice to swing wide around corners, use window glass for rearward visibility, and get something solid behind you when you pause.

All this may sound excessively furtive and melodramatic, but those who have cultivated what might be called a tactical approach to life find it neither troublesome nor conspicuous. And, like a fastened seat belt, a life jacket, or a fire extinguisher, it is comforting even when unnecessary.

Needless to say, no sensible person ever opens the door of his house without knowing who is knocking. If your entranceway does not permit visual evaluation of your caller, change it. The statistics may be against a threat waiting outside, but statistics are cold comfort after you discover that your case is the rare exception.

The foregoing suggestions are merely random examples of ways in which the principle of alertness is manifested. Situations are numberless, and specific recommendations cannot be made to cover them all. The essential thing is to bear always in mind that trouble can appear at any time. Be aware. Be ready. Be *alert*.

DECISIVENESS

PAUL KIRCHNER ©2005

DECISIVENESS

It is difficult for a domesticated man to change in an instant into one who can take quick, decisive action to meet a violent emergency. Most of us are unused to violent emergencies — especially those which can only be solved by the use of force and violence on our part — and these emergencies require a parturient effort of will to transform ourselves from chickens into hawks. Decisiveness, like alertness, is to some extent a built-in characteristic, but, also like alertness, it can be accentuated. In formalized combat it is supplied — or it should be — by appropriate orders from above. In cases of personal defense, it must be self-generated, and this is the problem.

When "the ball is opened" — when it becomes evident that you are faced with violent physical assault — your life depends upon your selecting a correct course of action and carrying it through without hesitation or deviation. There can be no shilly-shallying. There is not time. To ponder is quite possibly to perish. And it is important to remember that the specific course you decide upon is, within certain parameters, less important than the vigor with which you execute it. The difficulty is that the proper course of action, when under attack, is usually to counterattack. This runs contrary to our normally civilized behavior, and such a decision is rather hard for even an ordinarily decisive person to reach.

Short of extensive personal experience, which most of us would rather not amass, the best way to cultivate such tactical decisiveness is through hypothesis: "What would I do if . . . ?" By thinking tactically, we can more easily arrive at correct tactical solutions, and practice — even theoretical practice — tends to produce confidence in our solutions which, in turn, makes it easier for us, and thus quicker, to reach a decision.

English common law, the fountainhead of our juridical system, holds that you may use sufficient force and violence to prevent an assailant from inflicting death or serious injury upon you — or your wife, or your child, or any other innocent party. You may not pursue your attacker with deadly intent, and you may not strike an unnecessary blow, but if someone is trying to kill you, you are justified in killing him to stop him, if there is no other way. This is putting it about as simply as possible, and since the law here is eminently reasonable, the legal aspects of personal defense need not detain us in formulating a proper defensive decision. We must be sure that our assailant is trying to kill or maim us, that he is physically capable of doing so, and that we cannot stop him without downing him. These conditions can usually be ascertained in the blink of an eye. Then we may proceed. (Incidentally, rape is generally considered "serious injury" in this connection. A man who clearly intends rape may thus be injured or killed to prevent the accomplishment of his purpose, if no lesser means will suffice.)

So, when under attack, it is necessary to evaluate the situation and to decide instantly upon a proper course of action, to be carried out immediately with all the force you can bring to bear. He who hesitates is indeed lost. Do not soliloquize. Do not delay. Be *decisive*.

AGGRESSIVENESS

PRINCIPLE THREE:

AGGRESSIVENESS

In defense we do not initiate violence. We must grant our attacker the vast advantage of striking the first blow, or at least attempting to do so. But thereafter we may return the attention with what should be overwhelming violence. "The best defense is a good offense." This is true, and while we cannot apply it strictly to personal defensive conduct, we can propose a corollary: "The best personal defense is an explosive counter-attack." Those who do not understand fighting will at once suggest that numbers, size, strength, or armament must make this instruction invalid. They will insist that the aggressor will not attack unless he has a decisive preponderance of force. This is possible, but it is not by any means always, or even usually, true. Consider the Speck case, in which the victims outnumbered the murderer eight to one.

They disposed of far more than enough force to save their lives, but only if they had directed that force violently and aggressively against the murderer. This they failed to do. There are countless other examples.

The victory of an explosive response by an obviously weaker party against superior force is easy to observe in the animal world. A toy poodle runs a German shepherd off his property. A tiny kingbird drives off a marauding hawk. A forty-pound wolverine drives a whole wolf pack away from a kill that the wolves worked hours to bring down. Aggressiveness carries with it an incalculable *moral* edge in any combat, offensive or defensive. And the very fact that the assailant does not expect aggressiveness in his victim usually catches him unaware.

If the intended victim is armed, skill becomes a factor more critical than numbers. A man with a powerful, reliable sidearm, *who is highly qualified in its use,* can ruin a rifle squad at close range if he can seize the initiative by instantaneous aggressive response to a clumsily mounted attack. Of course such skill is rare, even (or perhaps especially) among our uniformed protectors, but it can be acquired. Great strides have been made in recent years in the theory of defensive pistolcraft. The results are available to respectable parties. But never assume that simply having a gun makes you a marksman. *You are no more armed because you are wearing a pistol than you are a musician because you own a guitar.*

In a recent case, a pupil of mine was assaulted by four men armed with revolvers as he drove into his driveway after a late party. Being a little the worse for wear, he violated (or just forgot) all the principles of personal defense but one and that was the principle of aggressiveness. At their first volley, he laid down such a quick and heavy barrage of return fire (twenty-two rounds in less than twenty seconds) that his would-be assassins panicked and ran. He did most things wrong, but his explosive reaction to attack certainly saved his life.

Now how do we cultivate an aggressive response? I think the answer is *indignation*. Read the papers. Watch the news. These people have no *right* to prey upon innocent citizens. They have no *right* to offer you violence. They are *bad people* and you are quite justified in resenting their behavior to the point of rage. Your response, if attacked, must not be fear, it must be *anger*. The two emotions are very close and you can quite easily turn one into the other. At this point your life hangs upon your ability to block out all thoughts of your own peril, and to concentrate utterly upon the destruction of your enemy. *Anger* lets you do this. The little old lady who drives off an armed robber by beating on him with her purse is *angry*, and good for her!

The foregoing is quite obviously not an approved outlook in current sociological circles. That is of no consequence. We are concerned here simply with survival.

After we have arranged for our survival, we can discuss sociology.

If it is ever your misfortune to be attacked, alertness will have given you a little warning, decisiveness will have given you a proper course to pursue, and if that course is to counterattack, carry it out with everything you've got! Be indignant. Be angry. Be *aggressive*.

SPEED

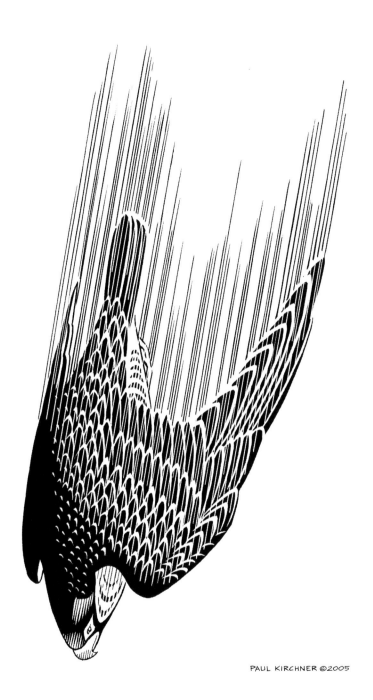

PAUL KIRCHNER ©2005

Principle Four:

SPEED

Speed is the absolute essence of any form of combat, from a fencing match to the Six-Day War. (Absence of speed is what history will probably decide caused us to lose in Vietnam.) Napoleon said, "I may lose a battle, but I will never lose a minute." Personal defense speeds this up. We must say, "I may lose this fight, but I will not lose this second!" Apparently overwhelming strength is of no importance if it is not brought to bear before it is pre-empted. In our Old West it was said, "Do unto others as they would do unto you, but do it first." Amen.

Here again this essay deals purely with defense, and neither law nor morality justifies our flattening someone just because we think he *might* attack us. However, on the very instant that we *know* that our assailant intends us serious physical harm, we must work just as fast as we can.

If he is holding us by threat of force, we have the edge of reaction time over him.

The stake in personal defense is your life. You cannot afford to play by sporting rules. Be fast, not fair. Be "offside" on the play. No referee will call it back.

The perfect fight is one that is over before the loser really understands what is going on. The perfect defense is a counter-attack that succeeds before the assailant discovers that he has bitten off more than he can chew.

Therefore, if you are attacked, retaliate instantly. Be sudden. Be quick. *Speed* is your salvation.

COOLNESS

PAUL KIRCHNER ©2005

Principle Five:
COOLNESS

You *must* keep your head. If you "lose your cool" under deadly attack, you will probably not survive to make excuses. So don't bother to improvise any . . . just *keep your head*. Anger, as long as it is controlled anger, is no obstacle to efficiency. Self-control is one thing the sociopath does not usually possess. Use yours to his undoing.

If you counterattack with your hands, use them carefully. (Remember that a blow with your closed fist to your enemy's head will almost always wreck your hand. A finger in his eye is easier, safer, and likely to be more decisive.)

If you improvise a weapon from objects at hand, use it in a way most likely to do damage without loss or breakage. The points of most improvised weapons, from umbrellas to fire pokers, are usually more effective than the edges, as they can be applied with less warning and without exposure during a "windup." A blunt point should be directed at the face or throat. Drive it carefully, coolly, and *hard*.

The optimum defensive arm is the heavy-duty pistol, though a shotgun may surpass it for home defense if there is sufficient warning. If you are fortunate enough to have access to any sort of firearm when under attack, remember that *it is as good as your ability to keep cool and shoot carefully*. My pupil, mentioned in Principle Four, did not shoot carefully, and he survived largely through luck alone, for his attackers shot just as sloppily as he did. But we cannot count on miserable marksmanship in our enemies. The sociopath is indeed usually a bad shot, but not always. Clyde Barrow was quite good.

Another student of mine did far better. To begin with, he heard the approach of the assassins' car in the cold grey light of dawn. He was alert even at that hour. He was on his feet immediately, pistol in hand. Through the blinds he saw two men coming rapidly up the walk to his door, one with a shotgun and one with a machine pistol. He decided that such a visit, with such equipment, at such an hour, needed no further explanation. He flung open the front door and went to work, and he remembered to remain *cool* and to shoot with *precision.* The two would-be murderers died in their tracks. The householder caught six pellets of bird shot in the leg. The attackers outnumbered and outgunned their proposed victim but they were defeated and destroyed by a man who did everything right.

When an expensively-trained police officer from one of the largest police departments misses a felon six times at a range of ten feet (and don't think this doesn't happen), his failure is not due to his technical inability to hit a target of that size at that distance, for he has demonstrated on the firing range that he can do so. His failure, and often his consequent death, is due to his lack of concentration upon his marksmanship — the loss of his cool.

The ability to remain cool under pressure comes more easily to some people than to others. But it is in no sense out of anyone's reach. In fact it is the first qualification of a man that Kipling calls for in his immortal poem *If*. It is illustrated beautifully every time you see a quarterback calmly select and hit his receiver while under the threat of more than one thousand pounds of rock-hard, cat-quick muscle only a step away. It's a matter of will. If you know that you *can* keep your head, and that you *must* keep your head, you probably *will* keep your head.

To train yourself to do this takes some thought. Certain kind of athletics are excellent — football, of course, in particular. Sailing, flying, motor racing, and mountaineering are also good. But in my opinion the best of them all is the hunting of medium and big game. "Buck fever" is a classic affliction, and a man who has conquered it can be guaranteed to shoot carefully under pressure. While it is true that a deer is not shooting back, this is less significant than might at first appear. The deer is about to vanish, and, odd as it seems, fear of sporting failure is usually greater than the fear of death. This startling point is easy to prove. The average competitive pistol shot works and trains far harder to earn a little brass cup than the average policeman works and trains to acquire a skill that can save his life.

Not all hunters make the grade — the woods are full of ditherers in red jackets. But the really expert hunter/rifleman is a very good man to have on your side.

Under any sort of attack, keep *cool*. And if you must shoot, shoot with *precision*.

RUTHLESSNESS

PAUL KIRCHNER ©2005

Principle Six:

RUTHLESSNESS

Anyone who willfully and maliciously attacks another without sufficient cause deserves no consideration. While both moral and legal precepts enjoin us against so-called "overreaction," we are fully justified in valuing the life and person of an intended victim more highly than the life of a pernicious assailant. The attacker must be stopped — at once and completely. Just who he is, why he has chosen to be a criminal, his social background, his ideological or psychological motivation, and the extent of injury he incurs as a result of his acts — these may all be considered at some future date. *Now*, your first concern is to stay alive. Let your attacker worry about *his* life. Don't hold back. Strike no more after he is incapable of further action, *but see that he is stopped*. The law forbids you to take revenge, but it permits you to prevent. What you do to prevent further felonious assault, as long as the felon is still capable of action, is justified. So make sure, and do not be restrained by considerations of forbearance. They can get you killed. An armed man, especially if he is armed with a firearm, is dangerous as long as he is conscious. Take no chances. Put him out.

If you must use your hands, use them with all the strength you possess. Tapping your assailant half-heartedly, for fear of hurting him, will indeed make him mad, and since he has already shown that he is willing to kill you, he may try even harder now that you have struck him a painful though indecisive blow. If you choose to strike, by all means strike *hard*.

This also applies to shooting. If you are justified in shooting you are justified in killing, in all but a few quite obvious circumstances. Don't try to be fancy. Shoot for the center of mass. The world is full of decent people. Criminals we can do without.

We often hear it said — especially by certain police spokesmen who, it seems to me, should know better — that in the event of victimization the victim should offer no resistance, for fear of arousing his assailant. Perhaps we should ignore the craven exhortation to cowardice made here. "Honor" may in truth be an obsolete word. So let us consider only results. The Sharon Tate party did not resist. The Starkweather victims did not resist. The LaBiancas did not resist. Mitrione did not resist. The next time some "expert" tells me not to resist I may become abusive.

Apart from the odds that you will be killed anyway if you submit to threats of violence, it would seem — especially in today's world of permissive atrocity — that *it may be your social duty to resist*. The law seems completely disinclined to discourage violent crime. The sociopath who attacks you has little to fear, at this writing, from either the police or the courts. The chief of police of our capital city has stated in print that, "The greatest real and immediate hazard that the hold-up man faces is the possibility that his victim may be armed and might shoot the criminal." (*U.S. News and World Report*, 8 December

1969, page 35.) The syntax may be a bit garbled but the meaning is clear. If violent crime is to be curbed, it is only the intended victim who can do it. The felon does not fear the police, and he fears neither judge nor jury. *Therefore what he must be taught to fear is his victim.* If a felon attacks you and lives, he will reasonably conclude that he can do it again. By submitting to him, you not only imperil your own life, but you jeopardize the lives of others. The first man who resisted Starkweather, after eleven murders, overcame him easily and without injury. If that man had been the first to be accosted, eleven innocent people would have been spared.

The coddling of murderers has brought us to an evil pass. If it is truly a wise and just policy (which we may have serious reason to doubt), leave it to the courts. When your life is in danger, for get it. If you find yourself under lethal attack don't be kind. Be harsh. Be tough. Be *ruthless.*

SURPRISE

PAUL KIRCHNER ©2005

Principle Seven

SURPRISE

This is put last on purpose, for surprise is the *first* principle of *offensive* combat. However, the privilege of striking the first blow is a luxury we must usually grant to our attacker, so in a sense there can be no strategic surprise in defense. But that does not mean that the defender cannot achieve *tactical* surprise. By doing what our assailant least expects us to do, we may throw him completely off. As we have seen, what he usually least expects is instant, violent counterattack, so the principle of aggressiveness is closely tied to threat of surprise.

One of the most hilarious episodes in cinema presents a bank teller debating the spelling of a written demand passed through the wicket by the bank robber. The whole affair shifts from banditry to an argument about whether the money can be handed over in the face of so badly constructed a missive. Pretty far-fetched, of course, but still stimulating. The unexpected is disconcerting. A disconcerted felon is momentarily less in charge of his own thoughts than the moment just before or just after. At that moment, his victim may be able to turn the tables.

On a realistic note, I can point out that in every single successful defense against violent attack that I know of — and I have studied this matter for decades — the attacker was totally surprised when his victim did not wilt. The speed, power, efficiency, and aggressiveness of the counterattack varied greatly, but the mere fact of its existence was the most elemental component of its success.

If you have friends in law enforcement, ask them to tell you the "April Fool" joke. It's a bit gamy for a publication of this sort, but it makes a point — and it is *very* funny. Its moral is the moral of this manual: The criminal does not expect his prey to fight back. May he never choose you, but, if he does, *surprise* him.

A FINAL WORD

There is a purpose to be served by this essay. The combination of modern medical science and the welfare state has brought about a condition of general overcrowding and boredom which, magnified by vast worldwide increases in population, has resulted in an unconscionable drop in personal safety. Before World War II, one could stroll in the parks and streets of the city after dark with hardly any risk — at least no more than was involved in driving on the highway. A young woman needed no escort. One could safely ask for help on the road. Meeting with another rifleman in the woods was occasion for comradeship rather than a red alert. This is true no longer. Today, and for the foreseeable future, the problem of personal risk is much more serious than of yore. Our police do what they can, but they can't protect us everywhere and all the time. All too often they cannot even protect themselves. Your physical safety is up to you, as it really always has been.

The principles herein enunciated are the result of a great deal of study and consultation, plus a fair amount of actual experience. Taken to heart, they may save your life. There is always an element of luck in any sort of conflict, and I know of no way to guarantee success in every instance. *What I do know, however, is that if the victims of the dozen or more sickening atrocities that have gained nationwide fame in recent years had read this book, and had heeded what they read, they would have survived those actions.* Additionally, a small but select number of goblins would not be alive today, bounding in and out of courts and costing us all money that could be much better spent.

George Patton told his officers, "Don't worry about your flanks. Let the enemy worry about *his* flanks." It is high time for society to stop worrying about the criminal, and to let the criminal start worrying about society. And by "society" I mean *you*.

JEFF COOPER is perhaps the nation's foremost authority on defensive weaponcraft. He is renowned not only for his practical instruction on marksmanship, safety, and firearm mechanics, but also for his groundbreaking ideas on proper defensive mental conditioning.

Principles of Personal Defense is a classic work. It presents the timeless theory of individual defensive behavior clearly, concisely, and practically. It deserves a place of honor in every library. All free people who aspire to stay that way should read, study, and share the wisdom found within these pages.

As Cooper wrote then, and believes to this day, it is safe to say that a decisive majority of murder victims would still be alive if they had read this short work *and heeded what they read*.